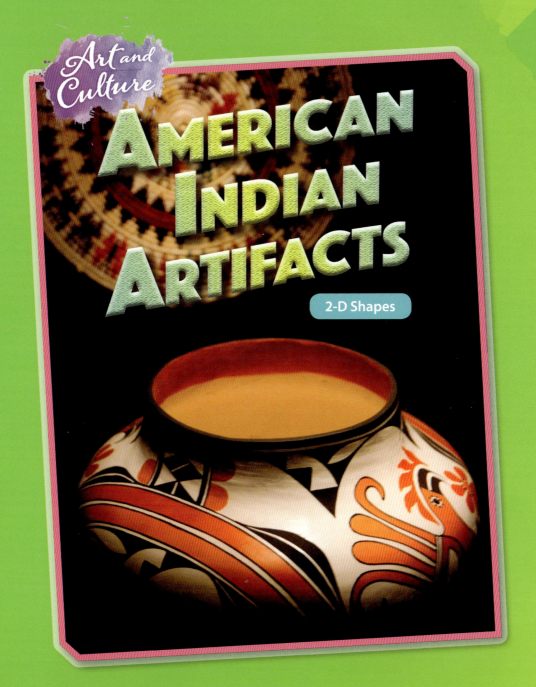

Art and Culture

American Indian Artifacts

2-D Shapes

Katie McKissick

Consultants

Michele Ogden, Ed.D
Principal
Irvine Unified School District

Colleen Pollitt, M.A.Ed.
Math Support Teacher
Howard County Public Schools

Karen Coody Cooper, M.A.
Cherokee Historian

Contributing Author
Dona Herweck Rice

Publishing Credits
Rachelle Cracchiolo, M.S.Ed., *Publisher*
Conni Medina, M.A.Ed., *Managing Editor*
Dona Herweck Rice, *Series Developer*
Emily R. Smith, M.A.Ed., *Series Developer*
Diana Kenney, M.A.Ed., NBCT, *Content Director*
Stacy Monsman, M.A., *Editor*
Kevin Panter, *Graphic Designer*

Image Credits: Cover and p.1 Dave G. Houser/Alamy Stock Photo; p.4 Buddy Mays/Alamy Stock Photo; p.7 (bottom) Antony Souter/Alamy Stock Photo; pp.8–9 RosalreneBetancourt 4/Alamy Stock Photo; p.11 (bottom) RosalreneBetancourt 5/Alamy Stock Photo; pp.12–13 Danita Delimont/Alamy Stock Photo; pp.13 (top), 22, 25, back cover National Museum of the American Indian, Smithsonian Institution; p.14 (top) Library of Congress [LC-USZ62-122131]; pp.14–15 Gary Cook/Alamy Stock Photo; p.15 Bag, c. 1900, Nez Perce, Denver Art Museum Collection: Gift of Dr. Charles J. Norton, 1986.261, Photograph courtesy Denver Art Museum; pp.16–17 Danita Delimont/Alamy Stock Photo; pp.17, 31 Birmingham Museum of Art; p.18 (inset) Wyoming State Museum, Department of State Parks and Cultural Resources; pp.18–19 Nancy G Western Photography, Nancy Greifenhagen/Alamy Stock Photo; p.19 Ron Bennett/Alamy Stock Photo; p.20 Library of Congress [LC-USZ62-105381]; p.21 Photo: Joshua Ferdinand, courtesy of The Nelson-Atkins Museum of Art, Object repository: State Historical Museum of Iowa; p.23 RosalreneBetancourt 9/Alamy Stock Photo; p.24 Maryann Groves/North Wind Picture Archives; p.27 (top) David R. Frazier Photolibrary, Inc./Alamy Stock Photo; p.29 Alison Jones/DanitaDelimont.com "Danita Delimont Photography"/Newscom; all other images from iStock and/or Shutterstock.

Library of Congress Cataloging-in-Publication Data

NNames: McKissick, Katie, author.
Title: Art and culture : American Indian artifacts / Katie McKissick.
Description: Huntington Beach, CA : Teacher Created Materials, 2018. | Includes index.
Identifiers: LCCN 2017012266 (print) | LCCN 2017029333 (ebook) | ISBN 9781480759466 (eBook) | ISBN 9781425855642 (pbk.)
Subjects: LCSH: Indian art--United States--Juvenile literature. | Indians of North America--Material culture--Juvenile literature. | Indians of North America--Antiquities--Juvenile literature. | Indians of North America--Museums--Juvenile literature.
Classification: LCC E98.A7 (ebook) | LCC E98.A7 M39 2018 (print) | DDC 970.004/97--dc23
LC record available at https://lccn.loc.gov/2017012266

Teacher Created Materials

5301 Oceanus Drive
Huntington Beach, CA 92649-1030
http://www.tcmpub.com

ISBN 978-1-4258-5564-2

© 2018 Teacher Created Materials, Inc.

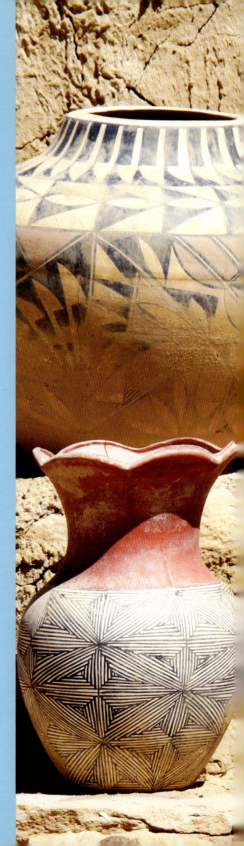

Table of Contents

Exploring the Past 4

Preserving History 7

Visiting a Museum 9

Gallery Walk 11

It's Your Turn 26

Problem Solving 28

Glossary 30

Index 31

Answer Key 32

Exploring the Past

The world is full of interesting people and places. Wherever you go, you can explore the culture of an area. You can study the art and architecture. You can listen to the music. You can eat the food. If you are lucky, you might even find a window into the cultures of long ago.

Throughout most of the United States, the culture you find is relatively modern. It is a young country. The history of the nation goes back only a few hundred years. That is a short amount of time compared with the rest of the world. But, that does not mean the land itself is without ancient history. People were on the land long ago. Some of their cultures live on.

The roots of culture throughout the Americas go deep. They thrive even today. In many ways, they are woven into the fabric of modern culture.

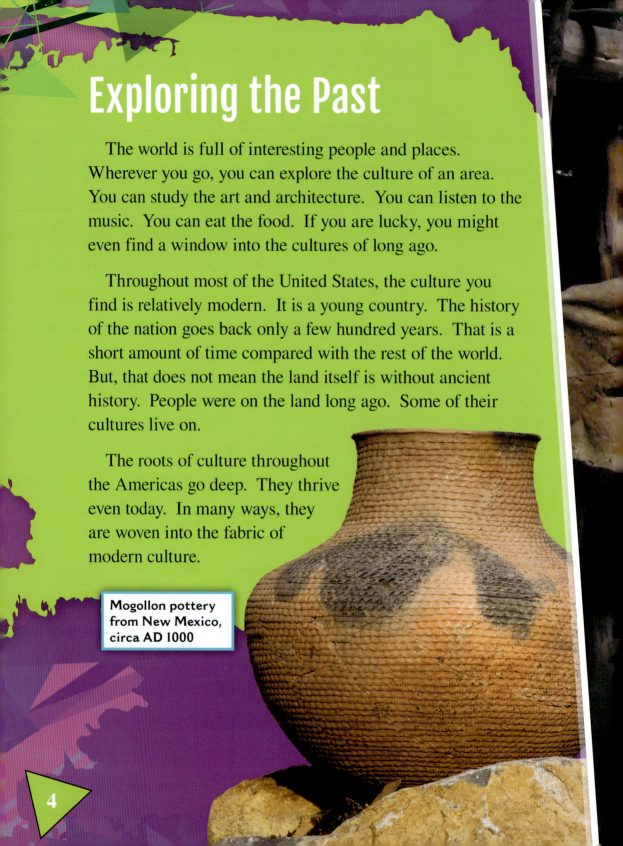

Mogollon pottery from New Mexico, circa AD 1000

painted hide and artifacts from a Great Plains tribe

National Museum of the American Indian in Washington, DC

Preserving History

If you know where to look, you can see traces of the cultures from long ago. Art and artifacts are in museums around the country. Some, such as the National Museum of the American Indian (NMAI), are dedicated to the preservation of art and culture. They bring to life the cultures of the **indigenous** people of North and South America. These museums house many works of art. Some of the art is hundreds or even thousands of years old.

All the pieces give us a window into the past. They show what life was like for people then. Some of those people may have stood on the very spot you stand now. The pieces tell a story of their daily lives. They tell stories, too, of ceremony and special times. They teach us about the people and their history. They make the past come alive.

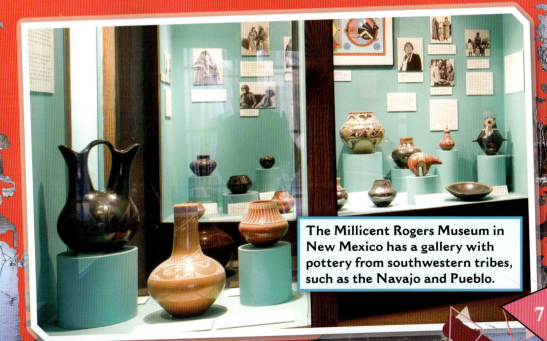

The Millicent Rogers Museum in New Mexico has a gallery with pottery from southwestern tribes, such as the Navajo and Pueblo.

A family tours an exhibit at NMAI in New York City.

Visiting a Museum

At most museums, there is a wealth of items to see. It can be overwhelming. It is best to pause and look at each item for a while. In this way, you can read about each piece. You can see how old the artwork is, and sometimes you can learn a little bit about the artist. Sometimes, a piece is so old that no one knows who made it. By taking a closer look, you can see tiny details the artist included in the piece. What colors and materials did the artist use? What shapes or **patterns** did the artist create?

Looking at each piece and learning about it can take quite a long time. To take it all in, you might even want to visit again. Exhibits at museums also change often. It can be a new experience every time you go!

A teacher and her students learn about American Indian artifacts at a museum.

Gallery Walk

NMAI has one of the largest collections of artwork in the world. It is in New York and Washington, DC. The pieces at both sites span thousands of years of history. The Heard Museum in Arizona is small but also hosts a wide array of art and artifacts. The Denver Art Museum is known for its vast collection. These are just a few of the museums about American Indians in the world. There are many more, large and small. Each one does its part to keep cultures alive.

Here and on the next pages, you can take a "gallery walk" through a museum. It is like taking a field trip through the pages of a book. Perhaps one day you can see these works of art in person. No matter how great a book is, it can never replace a firsthand visit!

To make the most of your tour, study the images on each page. Think about the art and what it says about the culture. And, appreciate the artist's work! It took great skill to make the stunning pieces you see here.

A visitor at NMAI uses a touch screen to learn more about an exhibit.

Acoma Jar

Pottery has been around for thousands of years. In the past, people used pottery for storage, cooking, and eating. People still use it for these things, but less so. Pottery is often decorative today.

The Acoma **tribe** in New Mexico made jars from clay. They made all pieces by hand. Their pottery is well known for its **geometric** designs.

Take a look at the details on this 100-year-old jar. There are designs in different colors. Orange and black are traditional tribal colors. Even today, Acoma artists use these colors in their art.

The design is made of different shapes. These shapes form a repeating pattern. But, each row is a little bit different from the others. The bottom and top rows have squares stacked like steps. The middle row has squares, triangles, and half circles. These shapes look like small flowers. The thin, slanted lines are called a hatching pattern. This pattern stands for rain in Acoma culture.

an Acoma pueblo village

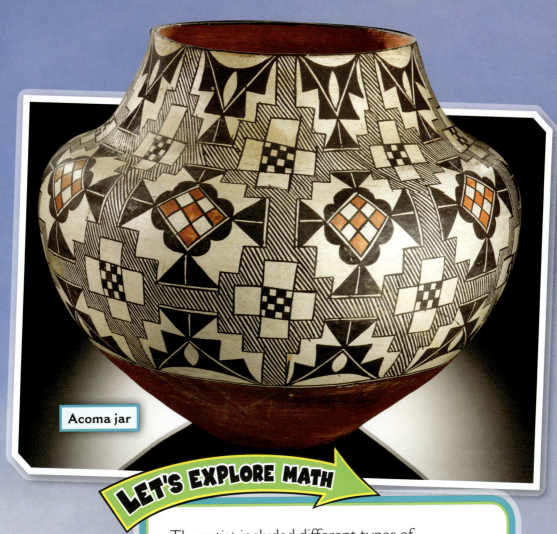

Acoma jar

LET'S EXPLORE MATH

The artist included different types of **quadrilaterals** on the painted jar. Find two of the quadrilaterals. How are these two polygons similar? How are they different?

A Nez Percé woman holds a similar bag in 1909.

Nez Percé Bag

The Nez Percé (PUHRS) tribe made all they needed from resources they found in nature. Its people often went to the Great Plains to hunt buffalo. They used the hides to make their homes and clothes. Buffalo hide is similar to leather. The women of the tribe adorned their clothes with items from nature. These included beads, cornhusks, and wool. They decorated other items, too, such as bags.

Bags were important to people of the Plains. The ability to easily carry things was useful for this culture. The people had horses and were often on the move. A Nez Percé artist made the bag shown below. It was most likely made in the Idaho area, more than 100 years ago.

The bag is decorated with an **intricate** pattern. Both style and function were important to the Nez Percé. Photos show that both men and women carried these bags. This one may have been used by different people to carry many needed things.

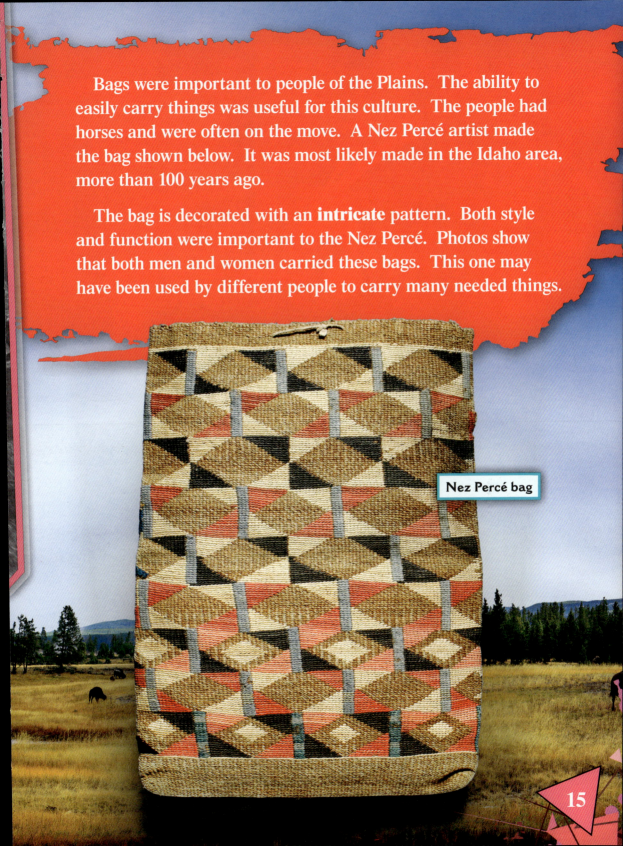

Nez Percé bag

A performer reenacts an Inka ceremony at the Festival of the Sun in Peru.

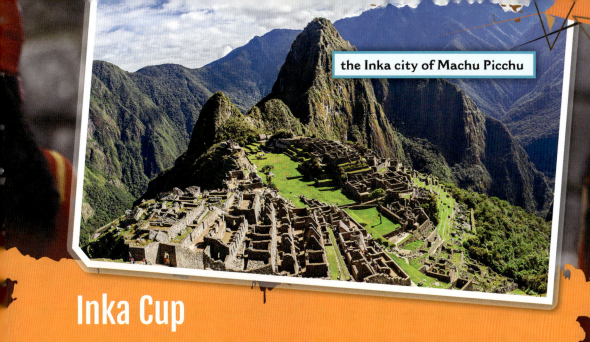

the Inka city of Machu Picchu

Inka Cup

American Indian pottery had uses beyond the home. This is a **ceremonial** drinking cup called a *qero*. It was only used for special events and celebrations. An Inka artist made it in the 1700s. The Inka lived high in the Andes Mountains in Peru. They had a huge empire. A ceremonial cup such as this one would have been used for large events.

The cup was made of wood covered in tree sap. First, the cup was carved. Then, the artist painted scenes on the outside of the cup. The artist used many colors to make the designs. The Inka often used geometric designs. The cup has many shapes as well as people painted on it. It is **preserved** very well. After all these years, you can still see the details.

Inka qero cup

Sioux Mask

Some museums are lucky enough to have horse masks. Horses are important to the cultures of many American Indian tribes. The tribes were called the "Horse Nation." The lives of the people depended on the use of their horses. Items made for horses were prized.

This mask is from South Dakota. It is thought to have been made around 1900. It may have been made for a Fourth of July event. It is one of about 50 such masks that still exist.

Sioux artists may have started making such masks as armor for their horses. This could have been inspired by the armor that Spanish conquistadors used. The masks are made of buffalo hide and covered in beads. The beads are used to form geometric designs and patterns. Colors help to form the patterns as well. The detail shows the respect the artist had for the horse wearing the mask.

An American Indian boy from South Dakota rides a horse that is wearing a decorative mask.

LET'S EXPLORE MATH

The stars on the Lakota horse mask are made of different types of triangles. Triangles can be classified by their sides and angles.

1. Draw and name a triangle with two sides of equal length and one **right** angle.

2. Draw and describe a **scalene** obtuse triangle.

3. Is it possible to draw an **equilateral** triangle that includes a right triangle? Explain your reasoning.

Sioux Blanket

Another piece you might see on a museum tour is a saddle blanket. This one is nearly 200 years old. It came from the Dakotas and was made by a member of the Sioux tribe. The blanket is quite large. It measures 64 inches (163 centimeters) in length.

Blankets such as this one are placed on a horse's back under the saddle to protect the horse. It also provides some cushion between the rider and the horse. Everyday blankets were not as fancy, though. This one was most likely made for a special occasion. It also showed the wealth of the owner.

This blanket is made from buffalo hide and wool. It is decorated with blue, black, and white glass beads. The beads make a pattern of lines and angled shapes. The pattern repeats around the edges of the blanket. A **complementary** pattern can be seen in the tabs at the blanket's four corners.

In earlier days, artists used porcupine quills instead of beads. The design on this blanket is similar to a style that might have been made using quills.

Sioux Indians sit on horseback on the Dakota plains in 1905.

Sioux saddle blanket

LET'S EXPLORE MATH

Parallel lines never intersect, or cross. Perpendicular lines intersect to form right angles that measure 90 degrees. What types of line segments are used in the pattern on this saddle? Explain your reasoning.

Plains Cree Saddle

A saddle such as this one would have been placed on top of a saddle blanket. But, this saddle is not from the Sioux tribe. A member of the Plains Cree tribe in Canada made it. It dates back more than 100 years.

LET'S EXPLORE MATH

The design on this saddle has triangles and quadrilaterals. There is an example of an **isosceles** right triangle, a square, a rectangle, a **rhombus**, and a **parallelogram**. Sort these polygons based on the properties of their sides and angles.

A mother and daughter from the Plains Cree tribe make beaded jewelry.

The saddle is made from hide, cotton, wool, and deer hair. It also includes glass beads, copper beads, and metal rings. Those materials were not usually used together. That makes this saddle fairly unique in its makeup. The artist would have had to work with care to get the glass, copper, and metal to fit together. In some ways, it would have been like working a puzzle. But, the artist had to create the pieces as well as the picture! It must have taken a great deal of time to make the geometric shapes that create the patterns. The design may look simple, but it is a stunning work of art. It is even more stunning when you consider the work that went into its creation.

Apsáalooke Case

The next art piece is a case used to store a headdress. A headdress is a crown of feathers. Only the most important members of a tribe (such as the chief) wear them. They are worn at special times, such as festivals and ceremonies.

This case comes from Montana. Someone in the Apsáalooke (ap-SA-ah-luk-ay) tribe made it more than 120 years ago. It protected the headdress when no one was wearing it. The artist used different kinds of hide and wool cloth to form the case. Then, the case was painted. The long strips, or **fringe**, are made from animal hide.

The case has shapes in red, green, blue, and yellow paint. Some of these shapes even join together to form new shapes. For example, in the middle of the case, two triangles join to form one square. By putting shapes in different places, an artist can create something completely new!

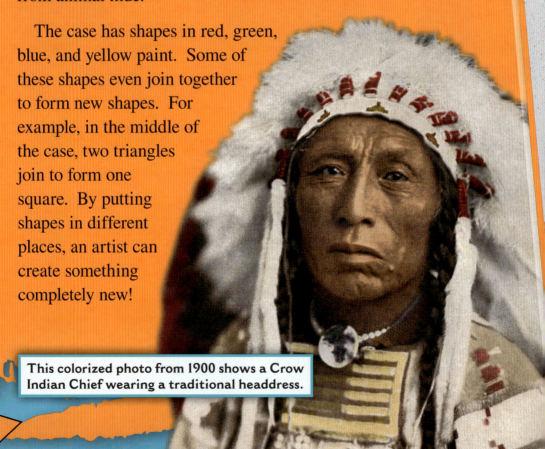

This colorized photo from 1900 shows a Crow Indian Chief wearing a traditional headdress.

Apsáalooke headdress case

LET'S EXPLORE MATH

Sometimes, artists use simple shapes to make other shapes. What shapes make the geometric figure below? What types of line segments and angles can be seen?

It's Your Turn

People have lived in the Americas for thousands of years. But, there is still much we do not know about the past. We can learn more and more by studying what people left behind.

Throughout the Americas, the influence of American Indian tribes is strong. These tribes date back for centuries. The work they create shows artistry and skill. By studying artifacts, we can see how those tribes have changed over time.

Today, artists continue to show their culture through their art. And you can be one of those artists! Try making something new. Bead a bag or make a mask for your pet. Create a pattern in fabric with natural materials you find. Who knows? Perhaps one day your work will be in a museum—or a book just like this one!

Navajo woven basket

Navajo decorative vase

A Pueblo boy from New Mexico crafts a dream catcher.

Problem Solving

Many artists use geometric shapes in their artwork. Sometimes these shapes form patterns. Colors can make patterns, too. Simple shapes can be combined to make other shapes.

Put your own artistic talent to work! Your task is to design a blanket using a variety of colors and shapes. You may even use a repeating pattern.

1. Draw each of the following shapes in your design. You may include more shapes than those listed here.

    - quadrilateral with at least 1 pair of parallel sides

    - quadrilateral with at least 1 pair of perpendicular sides

    - quadrilateral with at least 1 right angle

    - isosceles right triangle

    - equilateral triangle

    - scalene obtuse triangle

2. Choose two shapes from your design. Compare and contrast their properties to show how they are similar and different.

Glossary

ceremonial—used in or done at a formal event

complementary—going well together

equilateral—describes a triangle with 3 equal sides and 3 equal angles

fringe—a decorative border made from hanging strips or threads

geometric—made up of points, lines, and shapes

indigenous—being born in a particular place and having a sense of belonging there

intricate—complex, with many parts

isosceles—describes a triangle with two equal sides and two equal angles

parallelogram—quadrilateral with opposite sides equal and parallel, and opposite angles equal

patterns—sequences that repeat

pottery—objects made out of clay and then baked at hot temperatures to harden

preserved—kept safe from harm

quadrilaterals—polygons with four sides and four angles

rhombus—quadrilateral with all sides equal, opposite angles equal, and opposite sides parallel

right—measuring exactly 90°

scalene—describes a triangle with no equal sides or angles

tribe—a group of people who share the same language, customs, and beliefs

Index

Acoma, 12–13

Americas, 4, 26

Apsáalooke, 24–25

bag, 14–15, 26

bead, 14, 18, 20, 23

blanket, 20–22, 28

buffalo, 14, 18, 20, 24

case, 24–25

ceremony, 7, 24

cup, 17

Denver Art Museum, The, 11

gallery, 11

geometric, 12, 17–18, 23, 28

headdress, 24–25

Heard Museum, The, 11

Inka, 16–17

jar, 12–13

line, 12, 20–21, 25

mask, 18–19, 26

National Museum of the American Indian (NMAI), 6–7, 11

Plains Cree, 22–23

pottery, 4, 12, 17

saddle, 20–23

sinew, 24

Sioux, 18, 20–22

Answer Key

Let's Explore Math

page 13:
Answers will vary. Possible answer: square and rectangle; similar—4 sides; 4 right angles; opposite sides equal and parallel; different—square has 4 equal sides, while a rectangle has opposite equal sides

page 19:
1. Isosceles right triangle
2. 1 obtuse angle and 2 acute angles; no sides are the same length
3. No; equilateral triangles must have all angles equal, and it is impossible to draw a triangle where all 3 angles measure 90°.

page 21:
Parallel and perpendicular line segments; Explanations will vary, but may include that the line segments forming the sides are parallel, and the line segments forming the corners intersect at right angles.

page 22:
Groups will vary. Possible answer: all sides equal—square, rhombus

page 25:
Shapes: rectangles, right triangles, squares, trapezoids; squares, rectangles, and right trapezoids have both parallel and perpendicular sides; right triangles have perpendicular sides; trapezoids have 1 set of parallel sides; all have right (90°) angles except for the isosceles trapezoid

Problem Solving

1. Designs will vary, but should include at least one example of each polygon.
2. Answers will vary. Possible answer: square and isosceles right triangle; Similar—both have at least 1 right angle and at least 2 equal sides; Different—a square has 4 sides and 4 angles; a triangle has 3 sides and 3 angles